The Hamlet Inn

Kim Wedler

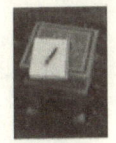

TSL Drama

First published in Great Britain in 2022
By TSL Publications, Rickmansworth

Copyright © 2022 Kim Wedler

ISBN: 978-1-914245-82-4

The right of Kim Wedler to be identified as the playwright/author of this work has been asserted by the author in accordance with the UK Copyright, Designs and Patents Act 1988.

All characters and events in this publication, other than those clearly in the public domain, are fictitious and any resemblance to actual persons, living or dead, is purely coincidental.

All rights reserved. No part of this publication may be reproduced, stored in a retrieval system or transmitted, in any form or by any means without the prior written permission of the publisher, nor be otherwise circulated in any form of binding or cover other than that in which it is published and without a similar condition being imposed on the subsequent buyer.

Rights of performance

Rights of performance for these scripts are controlled by TSL Publications [tslbooks.uk/Drama] which issues a performing licence on payment of a fee and subject to a number of conditions [specified on tslbooks.uk/Drama]. These scripts are fully protected under the Copyright Laws of the British Commonwealth of Nations, the United States of America and all countries of the Berne and Universal Copyright Conventions. All rights, including Online, Stage, Motion Picture, Radio, Television, Public Reading and Translation into Foreign Languages are strictly reserved. It is an infringement of the Copyright to give any performance or public reading of these scripts before the fee has been paid and the licence issued. The Royalty Fee is subject to contract and subject to variation at the sole discretion of TSL Publications. In Territories Overseas the fees quoted may not apply. A fee will be quoted on application to TSL Publications.

Cover courtesy of : Kim Wedler

Cast

Sheryl Bovey Tracey	– 50s, dressed in an expensive shirt, top button undone, beige linen slacks and canvas shoes, with a straw hat
Violet Hills	– small, older lady
Darlene Grockle	– petite, wearing tight fitting colourful clothes, deep south American accent
Eugene Grockle (Aaron Graceland)	– 50s, sparkly white jump suit, dark glasses and Elvis wig, deep south American accent
A. Pseudonym (Tony)	– stocky man, casually dressed
Paddy O'Doors	– 40s, weaing pale blue shirt and jeans
Leanne	– 20s, wearing hotel uniform, has a polaroid camera around her neck

Running Time
60 minutes

ACT 1

3 p.m. The setting is a small inn. A dripping tap is heard.

SHERYL: Good morning. Hamlet Inn. Torbay or not Torbay! [*Pause*] No, this is Torbay. It's just what we say on account of it being called "The Hamlet Inn" [*Pause*] Like Shakespeare? [*Pause*] To be or not to be? [*Pause*] No, I know Shakespeare wasn't born in Torbay. Yes, I know Agatha Christie was. I just don't think the "Sparkling cyanide hotel" or "The mouse trap" has quite the same ring to it. Roger Ackroyd died? Oh, I'm sorry to hear that. So, it's just Mrs Ackroyd, is it? [*Pause*] Oh, it's an Agatha Christie novel, no, I don't know that one. So, would you like to make a reservation? What name shall I put it under and when is it for?

Names, Victoria, Emma, Ginger, Mel B... Oh really! I do know you're naming the Spice Girls. [*Pause*] Heather, is that you? Oh, very funny. What's up? Don't tell me the hen weekend has been cancelled! [*Pause*] Oh, Jane can't come, well never mind. At least we won't have to listen to her going on about all her allergies and rashes. Why isn't she coming? She's worried about feathered pillows... And if the hotel has made sure there are no nuts on sight, or if the room is too high up. Well, best she stays at home then. [*Pause*] Why would Steve mind me going away? Have you met my husband? The football's on TV, the fridge is full of beer and reaPy meals [*Pause*] and I got him his favourite cereal [*Pause*] the one with the toy. He can't wait! [*Pause*] Ok, the house will look like we've been burgled, he won't have changed his socks, but so what? I'll be too busy having a wonderful weekend!

Listen, I better go, the owner has been sniffing around lately, and I've got "The Streatham Singers" staying this weekend. They usually stay at "The Royal Oak" but last week they hired it to a health and safety organisation, and they managed to set the conference room on fire! Typical! Yeah [*Pause*] cigarette or something. Oh, there's six of them and I've had to put three in each room... Why would they like that? [*Pause*] Singers! Not Swingers, they're a women's choir from Streatham performing at the pavilion.

Listen Heather, I better go. Can you hear that dripping? There's a hole in the roof and the owner is too tight to fix it!! He gave me a bucket to catch the drips in. It's pouring out there! Yes, ok, see you next weekend, I'll pick you up! Bye for now!

[*The door is opened, and the sound of a storm is heard, it is then slammed shut.*

A. PSEUDONYM enters, he is casually dressed, he has no luggage, just a small lunch box.]

SHERYL: Good afternoon sir, welcome to the Hamlet Inn. Have you got a reservation?

[*The stocky man enters, with a menacing stare, he has an East End accent.*]

PSEUDO: Yes.

SHERYL: Ok. [*Pause*] What is your name?

PSEUDO: A. Pseudonym.

SHERYL: Oh, yes. I saw that in the book. Very funny.

PSEUDO: Is it?

SHERYL: Cash or card?

PSEUDO: Erm.

SHERYL: Would you like breakfast in the morning?

PSEUDO: Erm.

SHERYL: Have you been to Torquay before?

PSEUDO: I erm. [*Angrily*] Is this a questionnaire?

SHERYL: Oh sorry.

PSEUDO: No, I'm sorry. Let's start again. Cash for the room.

[*He gets out a large wad of notes.*]

SHERYL: Goodness, what a lot of money. Did you rob a bank, Mr Pseudonym?

PSEUDO: No, who told you that?!

SHERYL: No one, it was just a joke.

PSEUDO: Oh, yeah, very funny. Sorry, I've just been cooped up for a while. In a confined space. [*Pause*] Cruise… Yes, I was on a cruise. A large ship, for a long time. It went from England to America. Everything was fine, people all dressed up, the band were playing. But then something terrible happened. We hit something large in the water, the boat started to sink, and we had to get off. So, I had to swim to shore. I'd met a beautiful lady on the boat, erm ship. I painted her portrait. I was determined to keep her safe. I managed to get that beautiful girl onto a large wooden door, and she floated across the sea to safety. [*Pause*] Rose was her name.

SHERYL: Isn't that just the plot of *Titanic*?

PSEUDO: Breakfast, sounds good.

SHERYL: Do you want to know what it is?

PSEUDO: I know what breakfast is.

SHERYL: No, I mean the menu.

PSEUDO: No, I like a good fry up!

SHERYL: Any allergies?

PSEUDO: [*Pause*] Hamsters and fuzzy felts.

SHERYL: No, I meant food allergies…

PSEUDO: Oh, I see, no I eat everything.

SHERYL: Ok, I'll make a note of that! [*Writes on a pad*] So anything for breakfast, [*Pause*] no allergies.

PSEUDO: Unless it's served by a hamster in a felt waistcoat.

SHERYL: Sorry?

PSEUDO: Just a joke, love.

SHERYL: Oh yes! Complimentary drinks in your room and also hot drinks to help yourself to in the breakfast room throughout the day. A selection of teas, coffees, hot chocolates etc.

PSEUDO: I'm Tony by the way, I don't mean to make you uneasy.

SHERYL: [*In a shrill, scared voice*] Oh no of course not!

[*The door is flung open, it is still raining.* BOVEY TRACEY *enters.*]

SHERYL: [*Overzealous*] Bovey, how lovely to see you!

BOVEY: I have only been for a short walk, if not more of a swim than a walk.

SHERYL: [*Over the top laughing*] Oh, Mr Tracey!

BOVEY: But I will play along... Oh, we meet again my angel. Simply divine. Quite bewitching. As Shakespeare once said, "If I could write the beauty of your eyes and number all your graces, the age to come would say, 'This poet lies; Such heavenly touches ne'er touch'd earthly faces'."

SHERYL: Oh, Bovey!

BOVEY: Shall I compare thee to a summer's day? Thou art more lovely and more temperate! Shakespeare, what a prolific writer! Elizabethan and Jacobean ages of British theatre! Oh, I hope I wasn't interrupting anything. Are you lunching?

[*Looks at the lunch box*]

A small luncheon, I see!

SHERYL: Oh no this isn't mine. No, you're not interrupting at all. I'm glad you're here!

BOVEY: Hello there, young man! You obviously know who I am, I need no introduction. Pray tell, who are you?

TONY:	Why do you want to know?
BOVEY:	It is customary when inhabiting such a quaint abode to exchange pleasantries. Wouldn't you agree?
TONY:	I'm Tony and you are...?
BOVEY:	Now don't be shy! I don't bite. I know it can be daunting, meeting me in the flesh, but just think of me as a normal man. That usually helps to get a grip of oneself. Yes, I am a renowned author, it is true! But I too, am able to talk to the simple folk of this town. Although I can hear you are not a local. If I put my detective hat on, I believe... You are from London. East End I believe!
TONY:	Yeah, so now I see why you speak funny. You fancy yourself as Shakespeare?
BOVEY:	Oh, no comparison! Shakespeare had more wit and wisdom with much better poetry. He also had more insight into characters' feelings and motives, and cleverer handling of light and dark, change of pace, and the weighing up of right and wrong.
	I write mysteries, crimes to solve!
TONY:	Crime you say?
BOVEY:	Yes, only just the other day in the small milkshake establishment a mere 200 yards away, I solved a crime.
TONY:	Really! What was it murder? Robbery, kidnapping!
SHERYL:	What in the Torre's place?
BOVEY:	I shouldn't say... but... It was sabotage!
TONY:	What did Saber Tagge do? Is he an Italian gangster?
BOVEY:	No sabotage is defined as: to deliberately destroy, damage, or obstruct something or someone especially for political or military advantage.
TONY:	Was Bo Jo there, putting more rules in place?
BOVEY:	Bo Jo? Is that some kind of circus character?

TONY: No Boris Johnson. I told him, I'm only wearing a mask in a shop, if I'm robbing it.

BOVEY: I don't really follow politics. I have enough fiction in my writing. Anyway, much worse than that.

SHERYL: Worse than murder, robbery, and kidnapping!

TONY: What, zombies coming in or hand grenades!!

BOVEY: I think you watch too many films!

SHERYL: As long as it wasn't an iceberg being thrown in!

TONY: Was that a dig at me!

BOVEY: It was... a case of jealousy...

TONY: Was the lady owner having an affair with a priest and fathered his love child?

SHERYL: That's *The Thorn Birds*!

BOVEY: No, a customer, who knew the owner was trying to ruin his business! I won't divulge anymore, as I may use the material for a new book.

TONY: A writer you say?...

BOVEY: As you really don't seem to know me, here is my card.

TONY: Bovey Tracey – "a delightful novelist, capable of mingling humour with sharp poignancy Tracey's narration, so elegantly laced with wit". Says *The Torquay Observer*, Winner of "Torquay's writers' competition 2018 and 2019". That's a lot to put on a business card! As well as email, telephone number and address. Oh and "Facebook". Very modern.

SHERYL: Facebook's hardly modern unless you've been locked away for 10 years. Have you been locked away for 10 years?

TONY: Women, eh Bovey? Always jumping to conclusions.

BOVEY: Erm, yes quite!

TONY: Anyway. I better take the key to my room.

SHERYL: Yes of course. Room 3. Turn left at the top of the stairs. Second door on the left.

TONY:	Thank you for your service. I'm meeting a friend here later, could you buzz me when he arrives? I'll just take this key and my lunch box.
	[*Takes the key and the lunch box*]
SHERYL:	Of course, I'll leave you to settle in. We offer all our guests a complimentary drink at 7 p.m.
TONY:	Cheers, see you later Bovey. Let's hope you don't have any more crimes to solve... Like the disappearing boiled egg at breakfast tomorrow, or the case of the missing white slice. [*Laughs loudly as he leaves*]
SHERYL:	I'm so glad you came in Bovey! I don't trust him. No luggage, wad of notes, lunch box, references to confined spaces.
BOVEY:	Oh, I'm sure he's just a working-class chap enjoying the Devonshire countryside. The fresh air obviously made him peckish! [*Pause*] If however, he has inhabited one of Her Majesty's establishment, maybe he has seen the error of his ways and has turned over a new leaf. In the spirit of foliage maybe we should offer him an olive branch. We are all God's creatures. We sometimes take a wrong path, but he must be commended for stepping back on the right road and continuing on a righteous and honest path. Who are we to judge?
SHERYL:	I suppose so.
BOVEY:	Oh, The wonder of you.
SHERYL:	Talking of Elvis songs. I've got an Elvis impersonator arriving here this afternoon!
BOVEY:	Oh, good grief. I cannot abide impersonators! Entertainment: impersonating a celebrity, making a mockery of their personal lives, copying behaviour patterns.
SHERYL:	What happened to not judging?... God's creatures...
BOVEY:	Before you know it, it's identity theft. And you know how I feel about any kind of theft.

SHERYL:	Yes absolutely... I did enjoy your last book Bovey. I lent it to all my friends.
BOVEY:	Oh, you are too kind Stacey.
SHERYL:	Sheryl. Is your room to your satisfaction? Number 6 as requested.
BOVEY:	Oh, wonderful!! It is such a quaint – garret?
SHERYL:	If that means loft then yes.
BOVEY:	A quiet space is all I have required, this summer!
SHERYL:	Shame about the rain today.
BOVEY:	I'm sure it will pass. A great while ago the world begun, With hey, ho, the wind and the rain. But that's all one, our play is done, And we'll strive to please you every day. *Twelfth Night* act 5, scene 1 Farewell, sweet maiden. I shall imbibe a pomegranate juice. Is it still...?
SHERYL:	In the breakfast room, just behind the arras. [BOVEY *exits behind the arras.* *A small older lady*, VIOLET, *is seen outside the main door. She calls through the letter box.*]
SHERYL:	[*To herself almost*] Why is she just standing outside? What's she doing now? She's opening the letter box.
VIOLET:	I can't get in!
SHERYL:	Push the door!
VIOLET:	Why isn't it opening?
SHERYL:	You have to push the door?
VIOLET:	Pardon?
SHERYL:	Push the door. [*Whispers*] Oh for goodness' sake! Can you shut the letter box, so I can open the door?
VIOLET:	Pardon?
SHERYL:	Can you shut the letter box, so I can open the door?

VIOLET:	It won't open.
SHERYL:	Stand back please.
	[SHERYL *opens the door; the heavy sound of rain is heard.*]
VIOLET:	Why wouldn't it open?
SHERYL:	You have to push it!
VIOLET:	Oh, it's not automatic, like the shops?
SHERYL:	No, it's a very old hotel.
VIOLET:	Oh sorry. We usually stay at "The Royal Oak".
SHERYL:	Oh, I see. You're the Singers from Streatham… Erm where are the rest of you? There's supposed to be 6 ladies.
VIOLET:	Oh yes, there are 6. They sent me in because, I'm the one in charge.
SHERYL:	Really?
VIOLET:	Yes, I'm Violet Hills. Also, they can't come in.
SHERYL:	Why not?
VIOLET:	They want to know if there is a ramp.
SHERYL:	A ramp?
VIOLET:	Yes, a disabled ramp. Well, not a disabled ramp, but a…
SHERYL:	Yes, I know what you mean. Are they all disabled?
VIOLET:	Well, Pearl and Ruby have walking frames. Edna has a stick, and Maude has a flask of whiskey that she drinks on the coach down, so she's quite unsteady at present. So, I'm the only able bodied one!!
SHERYL:	Yes, ok. We do have a ramp. I did explain on the phone that the rooms are up a flight of stairs.
VIOLET:	Yes, no problem.
SHERYL:	Are you sure?
VIOLET:	Oh yes. I found if I line them all up, single file with Maude at the front, Pearl takes a run up, using her stick like a pole vault she can usually use her body weight to

	shunt the rest along. That or tell them there's cream teas in the room. That usually does the trick!
SHERYL:	Oh, well as long as you're sure.
VIOLET:	Absolutely.
SHERYL:	So, the rooms are paid for. Is there anything else I can help you with?
VIOLET:	I think that will be all. We will probably get an early night.
SHERYL:	It's… 3 o'clock.
VIOLET:	Good grief, already! We are dirty stop outs!! A few rounds of scrabble and a practise for our concert!! [*Starts humming*]
SHERYL:	I'll get Mike to bring up your bags for you. He should be back from his break. He's had 15 minutes, although I get the feeling, he thinks 6 hours is his break, with a 15-minute work period.
VIOLET:	Oh dear.
SHERYL:	I'll buzz him, if he's asleep in the utility room, it will wake him up.
	[SHERYL *goes onto the phone, it rings for a while, she smiles at* VIOLET *willing it to be answered.*]
SHERYL:	Oh, Mike. I've got luggage for you to take up please. [*Pause*] Yes, now. [*Whispers*] No, not after your pot noodle. Now! [*Pause*] No it's not the Americans. He'll follow you up!
VIOLET:	Wonderful!
SHERYL:	Here are your keys, room 1 and 2. Up the stairs. Either set, by the ramp or here by the main entrance. Complimentary drinks in your room. Breakfast 8–10 a.m. Or in your room. We can send up a continental.
VIOLET:	Oh, is that the waiter, is he French?
SHERYL:	Sorry?
VIOLET:	The continental.

SHERYL: Oh no I was referring to the breakfast, croissants, and pastries. Mike will probably bring that up.

VIOLET: Is he continental?

SHERYL: No, he's... just... judgmental. I'll leave you to it. Just to let you know, we offer all our guests a complimentary drink at 7 p.m.

VIOLET: Oh, well I am quite partial to a sherry. Yes, I will keep awake for that!

[*Goes off singing, "Lily the Pink".*]

VIOLET: [*Exits to the back*]. I'm coming everyone!!

[SHERYL *crosses names out on her guest list.*]

SHERYL: So, "The Streatham singers" in rooms 1 and 2. Tony in room 3, Bovey in room 6. The Grockles AKA Elvis impersonator and wife in room 4. Paddy O'Doors in room 5. Full house!!

[*The door is flung open, it is still raining. The GROCKLES enter.*]

EUGENE: Well, howdy Mumma, is this the heartbreak hotel?

DARLENE: [*Laughs*] Oh honey, you kill me!!

SHERYL: Mr and Mrs Grockle I presume!

DARLENE: How did you guess?

SHERYL: I had my suspicions.

EUGENE: [*Singing "Suspcious Minds"*] "We can't go on together! With suspicious minds..."

DARLENE: [*Sings*] With suspicious minds!!

SHERYL: Ok. Well welcome to "The Hamlet Inn".

DARLENE: It's so quaint.

SHERYL: We think so.

DARLENE: Well, we were warned about the UK weather. So rainy!! It got us all shook up!

EUGENE: [*Sings*] "All shook up". Like my wife said, it's our first visit to the UK.

DARLENE:	We got the phone call from Eugene's agent, we were so excited!!
	We couldn't wait for the fragrant cubes of jello and to get one of those cute little red hats! [*Pause for laugh*]
EUGENE:	But when we got the email, we realised we'd misheard him on the phone!
DARLENE:	We thought he said Turkey!!
EUGENE:	And it was Torquay!!... Stupid spelling of key! What kinda key is it?
SHERYL:	No, it's Quay, like quayside. It's the shore part of the harbour. It's where the ships dock.
EUGENE:	[*Breaks into song*] "Bridge over troubled waters".
SHERYL:	Ok, so you are in room 4, up the stairs, all the way to the right. Will you be wanting breakfast in the morning?
DARLENE:	Maybe something light!
EUGENE:	We've had a whole weekend of eating already and it's only Saturday!
DARLENE:	[*Laughs*] Eugene had a show in Newquay [*pronounces New Kway*]
SHERYL:	Newquay.
DARLENE:	Another key? [*Pause to digest*] Anyway, we were sitting by the coast and we wanted to try a local food product, so, we had a "Cornish Pasty" Oh my! They say us Yanks have big portions. It covered the plate!!
EUGENE:	I didn't know whether we should eat it or use it as a door stop.
DARLENE:	[*Laughs*] She'd made it with too much pastry, but rather than throw any away, she kinda hemmed it all at the top and ruffled it!
SHERYL:	Well, that is how they do it!
DARLENE:	It was so heavy!!
EUGENE:	Tell her about the other one honey!

DARLENE: The other one honey?

EUGENE: The tea.

DARLENE: Oh yeah. On a visit to Port Isaac. Where they make the Doc Martins. Although I never saw a single pair. [*Pause*] We wanted a drink.

EUGENE: This is funny!

DARLENE: So, I wanted a tea, it said cream tea. So, I thought it meant a tea with creamer. But guess what?

SHERYL: Enlighten me.

DARLENE: It was a *huge cake,* cut in half with jelly and cream! It was huge!

EUGENE: Huge!!! Like a bath sponge!

DARLENE: I was frightened I was going to sink to the bottom of the ocean!

EUGENE: But I said "It's now or never", give it to me! [*Continues to sing!*]

DARLENE: And he ate it all!!

EUGENE: It was nice enough, but a bit too sweet!!

DARLENE: So, in answer to your question about breakfast, maybe just some sausage and syrup!

SHERYL: I will see what I can do! Complimentary drinks in your room. We offer all our guests a complimentary drink at 7 p.m.

EUGENE: Well, that's mighty fine!

SHERYL: Here is your room key. Room 4 all the way round to the right!

EUGENE: Thank you kindly.

[EUGENE *and* DARLENE *exit,* EUGENE *singing "You were always on my mind".*]

SHERYL: Right well! Just Paddy O'Doors to come now. Maybe while it's quiet, I can give Steve a call. [*Dials phone*] Steve… I'm at work, where did you think I was? No, the hen weekend's next weekend. [*Pause*] Why? You haven't invited the lads around have you? I told you I was away *next* weekend. Well phone them up and tell them *next* weekend. Or you can meet them down the pub. [*Pause*] It's been really busy today, so I just want to get home later and put my feet up! About 8 o'clock, traffic permitting. [*Pause*] What are you wearing? [*Pause*] Nothing but a smile?... No, I didn't mean like that! Don't you remember my mum's popping around with a yucca and she doesn't want to encounter you sitting in your underpants. [*Pause*] A take away, that sounds nice! [*Pause*] Hang on, I left a casserole in the fridge for us tonight! [*Pause*] What all of it!! You pig! [*Pause*] Don't you remember me telling you... No of course you don't. Yes, Ok, a takeaway would be nice. Oooh Chinese, yes usual. Oooh and those little dumplings we like, oooh and the extra-large chicken Saturday's. I think if you spend a certain amount you get the prawn crackers for free!! Yes, that sounds lovely! See you later, don't forget to put some clothes on and not too much Xbox!! Yes, you're forgiven! See you later! [*Kiss noise down the phone.*]

[*The door is flung open, it is still raining. PADDY O'DOORS enters. He knocks on the door then slightly opens it. He carries 4 plastic bags, with clothing in them.*]

PADDY: Knock. Knock.

SHERYL: Sorry.

PADDY: You're supposed to say who's there. We'll try again! Knock. Knock.

SHERYL: Who's there?

PADDY: Ireland!

SHERYL: Ireland who?

PADDY: Ireland you money if you promise to pay me back.

SHERYL: Paddy O'Doors I presume?

PADDY: No flies on you!

SHERYL: Good Journey?

PADDY:	I got the ferry and then the coach. The coach driver kindly stopped outside. He was struggling to find a parking space. I said, Lord! If you open a space up for me, I swear I'll give up the Guinness and go to mass every Sunday. Suddenly, the clouds part and the sun shines on an empty parking spot. So, I said, "Never mind, I've found one!"
SHERYL:	Really?
PADDY:	No, I don't pray.
SHERYL:	No, I meant about the rain, has it stopped?
PADDY:	No, it's desperate out.
SHERYL:	Sorry your stay this summer is in the rain!
PADDY:	No, it's fine. In Ireland it rains all the time. The only way we know it is summer, is because the rain is warmer!
SHERYL:	How was the ferry crossing? It must have been choppy!
PADDY:	Oh, it was! I walked up to the bar to steady me nerves, and then I let go of the bar and went up to get a drink!
SHERYL:	Well, Mr O'Doors there's a complimentary drink at 7 p.m. Now breakfast is at 8 a.m. Before I forget... Oh dear I did forget to tell the others... We have no toast. The toaster keeps short circuiting. [*Whispers almost to herself*] I really must throw it away. It causes the whole circuit box to trip. Many a times have I been in the breakfast room and I've had to clamber about in the large cupboard. Switching it back on!!!
PADDY:	Do you do eggs for breakfast?
SHERYL:	Yes, we do.
PADDY:	No eggs please. Do you do bacon for breakfast?
SHERYL:	Yes, we do.
PADDY:	No bacon please.
SHERYL:	Beans?
PADDY:	Yes... no beans I'm a vegetarian!
SHERYL:	But...

PADDY:	Vegetarian, I don't eat vegetables.
SHERYL:	Maybe it would be better if you tell me what you *would* like.
PADDY:	Oh yes, what a good idea! What a clever lady! Yes.
SHERYL:	[*Pause*] So?
PADDY:	Oh yes, I'll have beef sausages, in white bread and a pint of Guinness.
SHERYL:	We don't have Guinness for breakfast.
PADDY:	Oh yes, what was I thinking. A whiskey.
SHERYL:	We don't do alcohol with breakfast.
PADDY:	Oh, is it religious reasons? On account of what you believe.
SHERYL:	No, on account of it being 8 a.m.
PADDY:	I don't really see where we're going here.
SHERYL:	Here are the keys to room 5.
PADDY:	Thank you. Oh, I have a friend staying. Erm Tony. I'm not sure of his surname.
SHERYL:	Oh yes. I'll check if he's in his room.
PADDY:	Oh, that sounds grand!
SHERYL:	I'll just dial Mr Pseudonym, for you.
PADDY:	Ok, and then Tony.
SHERYL:	That *is* Tony.
PADDY:	Oh, yes of course. I forgot!!
SHERYL:	Hello there Mr Pseudonym, Mr O'Doors is here for you. [*Pause*] Ok, will do.
	[*Into the phone*] Ok, thank you. [*To* PADDY] He's on his way!
PADDY:	Lovely painting that! I love sunflowers!
SHERYL:	Are you a painter?
PADDY:	Yes.
SHERYL:	Do you paint landscapes or still life?

PADDY: Ceilings.

[TONY *appears with the lunch box.*]

TONY: Great to see you again Paddy!

PADDY: Hello my friend, come and take a seat! I just wanted to check the… [*Looks over and sees that* SHERYL *is listening*] We don't want to keep you from any jobs you may have.

SHERYL: Oh no, I'm fine. [*Phone rings, it is an internal ring*] Sorry Mr Grockle? Something tasted odd with the complimentary mini bar. We don't offer a mini bar [*Pause*] So what have you been drinking? Oh, no those were the complimentary bubble baths, not a complimentary mini bar. Oh dear. Ok, I'll bring you up a jug of water. I'll also bring up some Alka Seltzers. Alka… never mind, I'm on my way. Must go, bit of a… liquid emergency.

[*Exits*]

PADDY: Tony, what's with the lunch box?

TONY: Oh, just my little secret box.

PADDY: For what?

TONY: Well, people think I have my lunch in here.

PADDY: So, you don't.

TONY: No, [*Whispers and looks around*] it's my passport, pen knife and a torch. It's an emergency kit.

PADDY: Oh, ok. My emergency kit is me hip flask of whiskey, but each to their own.

TONY: So, this is legit then, this job of yours?

PADDY: 111% absolutely. Building flats near Totnes. Good honest work, I promise you!

TONY: Alright. Because I want to keep my nose clean from now on!

PADDY: To be sure!

[VIOLET *appears, looks nervously around.*]

VIOLET:	Helloo! Excuse me gentlemen, have you seen the receptionist?
TONY:	She had to go and sort out a couple of the guests. Some sort of bubble bath drinking emergency.
VIOLET:	Oh dear, that's awful.
PADDY:	Yes, drinking bubble bath is a step too far even for me.
VIOLET:	I really wanted an early morning call. We have a singing rehearsal at 8 a.m. sharp. I don't like to oversleep... Never mind, I will try again later. I love the décor in this hotel. That exquisite painting, I love sunflowers. Let me take a closer look at this music box.
	[*She suddenly catches sight of the sunflower painting in a frame hanging on the wall.*]
	Oh, my this is a Gibbons!
PADDY:	Oh, I know it's bad, but I don't think a monkey did it!
VIOLET:	No, the great "Grinling Gibbons". He was given his first royal commission in 1675, when he was hired by Charles II to produce decorative carvings for Windsor Castle.
	Marvellous!
TONY:	Do you know what she's talking about?
PADDY:	Haven't got a clue, I stopped listening.
VIOLET:	A piece like this can be worth £30,000!
PADDY:	I heard that!
VIOLET:	I'll say good evening to you all. Oh, Sheryl did you sort out your troubled guests?
	[*She heads up to her room.* SHERYL *returns, humming.*]
SHERYL:	Tragedy averted! Oh, Mrs Hills, do you need me?
VIOLET:	Yes, now what was it...? Oh, do you know it's gone out of my head. I may remember later.
TONY:	[*Whispers*] Mrs Hills is from a singing group, load of old dears up there trying to sing either that or one's stuck in the fold up bed [*Sniggers*]

PADDY:	[*Winks and speaks in a loud over exaggerated voice*] That is terrible!!
SHERYL:	Is something wrong? The bucket hasn't overflowed again has it?
PADDY:	No, it's the old ladies from upstairs. Tony said one is screaming like a banshee! I hope she hasn't got stuck in the fold up bed! I'd go and help myself, but my manly physique may make her nervous.
TONY:	I didn't say...
PADDY:	I wouldn't want anyone to suffer!
SHERYL:	Oh dear. No, you're right I'll go. If anyone comes in, just say I'll be down shortly. It should be fine. All the guests are in now.
PADDY:	You can trust us!
	[SHERYL *goes to leave; she stops and goes behind the counter. She is holding a tool bag, with a crowbar sticking out.*]
SHERYL:	Just check the bucket doesn't overflow!
PADDY:	Will do!!
TONY:	Do you think she'll be alright?
PADDY:	What, the receptionist? I think she's got a mean side to her. Probably gets on the wrong side of everyone. Probably even her shadows pushed off!!
TONY:	No, the old lady.
PADDY:	I made it up you eejit!! [*Pause*] So what do you think about the painting?
TONY:	It's ok, although I prefer roses than sunflowers. I find them a bit creepy, like in those horror films. Tall and looming.
PADDY:	No, that painting isn't what she was looking at, I can see from here it's signed Van Goff.
TONY:	Oh, I've heard of him. He's a famous painter.
PADDY:	Yes, but he didn't paint that!

TONY:	How do you know?
PADDY:	He's signed it and Van Goff is not the right spelling. Even I know there's no "f" in gogh!
TONY:	So, what?...
PADDY:	It's the music box underneath on the mantel piece! She was talking about that! Worth £30,000 she said!!
TONY:	Well yeah but... Oh no! I know what you're thinking.
PADDY:	A sure thing. Little extra cash.
TONY:	Oh no, my girlfriend said this time she'd definitely leave me, and I don't want that. She makes the best bangers and mash!
PADDY:	Think of the restaurants you could take her to. The clothes she could buy. I bet she'd love that!
TONY:	I suppose so but...
PADDY:	Good. Now this is the plan. Now it's just after 4 p.m. Everyone will come down at 7 p.m. for drinks. That's just over two hours' time.
TONY:	To do what?
PADDY:	I'm thinking... Yes, we can go into the town and get a cheap little music box. I saw a shop on the way here. Oh, this is brilliant! I remember it's next to the pub. We buy the box!
TONY:	And then what?
PADDY:	Then after a couple of pints we come back, just before 7 p.m. So, at 7 p.m., everyone will be down here. Apart from you.
TONY:	Where will I be?
PADDY:	In your room.
TONY:	Where will you be?
PADDY:	Down, here ready to turn the lights off by tripping the fuse.
TONY:	Do you know how to do that?

PADDY: Yeah, it was one of the courses we could take inside. [*Pause*] What did you take?

TONY: Needlework.

PADDY: Then you can swap the real music box with the fake one!

TONY: The fake one?

PADDY: Yes, the music box we have bought from the souvenir shop. Then we will come up with a signal, to say you have swapped it and then I will turn the lights back on. Then everyone will go to bed after the ordeal and in the morning we will leave. Have you got it?

TONY: Ok. Do we need code words? I think it will help.

PADDY: Ok, when I turn off the lights. I'll say erm [*Pause*] erm England can't make boiled cabbage soup like my Ma, it seems fake. That's for you to swap it with the fake one. You can then say. "It's all good. The real one is as good as my pizza". Meaning you've swapped the box.
Then when the lights are back on. I will say goodnight all.

TONY: What's that code for?

PADDY: Nothing.

TONY: How do we flog it; I don't know anything about antiques.

PADDY: Do you remember Cobbler?

TONY: Who?

PADDY: Cobbler... Cement shoes, concrete boots. Swimming with the fishes?

TONY: [*Pause*] Oh my God!!

PADDY: He owned a string of antique shops. Alright some were a front for other businesses, but he knows people. He's out of prison, so he'd know how to flog it for us.

TONY: £30,000!

PADDY: Yeah, so split three ways that's ... 12,000 for me and Cobbler and 6,000 for you.

TONY: Hold up!

PADDY: What?

TONY: How did you know we can trust "The cobbler"?

PADDY: Let's just say he owes me a favour!

TONY: Sounds like a plan!

PADDY: £12,000. Nice little earner for hardly any effort. I wish all jobs were this easy. Looks like, I'm that much closer to me new conservatory!

TONY: Alright, you've convinced me!

PADDY: Let's have a drink on it. I saw a great little pub on the corner. We'll be back later to have the "cabbage soup".

TONY: I don't like... Oh yeah.

PADDY: My God and they say the Irish are thick!!

[PADDY and TONY start to leave.

BOVEY TRACEY appears.]

BOVEY: Gentleman, gentleman are you off for a stroll?

TONY: Oh, Mr Tracey, I didn't see you there.

BOVEY: I was behind the arras.

PADDY: I'll get behind your arras in a minute?

BOVEY: No, no, behind the tapestry, the arras.

TONY: We hope we didn't disturb you with all our talking.

BOVEY: Oh, my dear fellow, absolutely not. I have only just removed the cotton wool from my ears.

TONY: Cotton wool.

BOVEY: Yes, a touch of earache unfortunately. So, I heard nothing.

PADDY: Oh, that's grand... I mean, that we didn't disturb you. Not that you have earache.

BOVEY: Yes, I understand. I shall let you go on your merry way.

TONY: Cheers.

[PADDY *and* TONY *exit.*]

BOVEY: As Dickens once said, "I hope that real love and truth are stronger in the end than any evil or misfortune in the world."

Act 2

6.45 p.m. The door is flung open, it is still raining. LEANNE *enters. She has a polaroid camera around her neck.*

LEANNE: Sorry I'm late Sheryl. I got caught up in the rain... Sheryl? [*Looks around*] That's strange.

[BOVEY TRACEY *enters, from his room.*]

BOVEY: Oh, my dear Lesley...

LEANNE: It's Leanne.

BOVEY: "The poet's magic has laid open the depths of woman's nature, lovely and exquisite emotion, capturing her femininity."

LEANNE: Thank you Mr Tracey.

BOVEY: I must say, in a world of sensationalized automated newsfeeds and fake news, old souls are now more needed than ever. Old Soul!!

LEANNE: Sorry... I...

BOVEY: The use of the polaroid camera, rather than digital.

LEANNE: Oh, yes definitely. Did you know, the first Polaroid camera, called the Model 95, and its associated film went on sale in 1948 at a department store in Boston.

BOVEY: Oh, my dear, I see history fascinates you. Somehow, you ache to be a part of an era where life was simpler, where people are more connected by life rather than technology. And this is the way I want to live my life, too. Rather than dealing with the superficialities of mainstream society, an old soul has deeper interests.

LEANNE: In recent years, instant cameras have swung back into fashion, Mr Tracey.

BOVEY:	Oh, how true! You have wisdom beyond your years. You are more enlightened than others of your age.
LEANNE:	You are very kind!
BOVEY:	Do you have any photos about your person, that I could see?
LEANNE:	Oh, yes always. Mostly from last week when we had, oh what do you call it… Oh yes, sunshine. [*Produces a handful of photos.*]
BOVEY:	Mm, extraordinary, very good. You have a good eye for capturing the human form. Could I ask you to take a few of the guests tonight Linda?
LEANNE:	Leanne, yes of course.
BOVEY:	Now if you would excuse me, I am going to get another glass of pomegranate juice from behind the arras. As you can see, I have brought down a pencil and paper to make some notes. The light at this time of the evening is quite wonderful in the breakfast room.
LEANNE:	Oh yes of course Mr Tracey.
	[BOVEY *exits.*
	SHERYL *appears, very flustered.*]
SHERYL:	Any phone calls?
LEANNE:	Erm…
SHERYL:	Emptied the bucket?
LEANNE:	Well, I…
SHERYL:	Oh Leanne, you've only just arrived, haven't you?
LEANNE:	Sorry, I got caught up…
SHERYL:	Taking photos no doubt. Listen, I know this is just a summer job until you start your photography course, but you have to be on time! You should have been here at six!
LEANNE:	Why, what happened?
SHERYL:	Leanne! Just because you're my niece you still have to follow the rules. I can't cover for you again. You *have* to

	be on time. I really had to work on Mr Abbot to give you the job!
LEANNE:	I'm sorry. I'll make a real effort next time. Where were you anyway?
SHERYL:	Well, one of the guests said he thought he'd heard one of the Streatham Singers, howling as if in pain. At first, I thought it might just be their singing, but I thought I'd better check.
LEANNE:	And!
SHERYL:	Well, Edna, had managed to have got herself folded up in the sofa bed. You know that old white one? Not the lady, the bed. All I could see was her head sticking out, all red and flustered. It was like seeing a gigantic hot dog in a roll.
LEANNE:	OMG!!
SHERYL:	So, I calmly talked to her, to check she was alright, and she told me, she'd taken her cup of tea in bed with her.
LEANNNE:	So, what happened?
SHERYL:	Well, at first, I thought, what should I do? The tea might have scalded her, the cup might have broken and cut her.
LEANNE:	Go on!
SHERYL:	Well first I asked one of the other ladies, Maude, if she would help. Well, she was out cold.
LEANNE:	Not...
SHERYL:	No, not dead, dead drunk on whiskey. So, then I asked the other lady to help, She, told me she suffered from weak wrist syndrome!
LEANNE:	So, what happened next?
SHERYL:	Well... All of a sudden, the bed flung open, she'd also taken her stick to bed and it somehow levered itself on the open mechanism.
LEANNE:	Was she ok?

SHERYL:	Yes, a little shaken, but ok. Luckily the tea had already been drunk, the cup seemed to have found a space unharmed.
LEANNE:	Thank goodness.
SHERYL:	But then, Maude woke up and started yelling at the poor woman.
LEANNE:	Why?
SHERYL:	Maude said that the pearl necklace that Edna was wearing was hers. She then pulled it off her! Maude went into the toilet and locked herself in!
LEANNE:	Unbelievable.
SHERYL:	Edna was shaking after being folded in the bed and having a necklace ripped off her. I calmed her down and told her I'd give her compensation.
LEANNE:	How much?
SHERYL:	Well fortunately, as she sat composing herself. She heard Mr Grockle go past, he's the Elvis impersonator.
LEANNE:	And?
SHERYL:	Well, at first, she thought she heard a ghost. [*Puts on an old lady's voice*] I can hear Elvis!! But when I told her it was just an impersonator, she said she'd like some tickets for his show. So that was that.
LEANNE:	What about Maude, the old lady stuck in lavatory?
SHERYL:	Well, I knocked on the door and she was sparko on the toilet.
LEANNE:	What an event!
SHERYL:	That's not even all of it!
LEANNE:	No way!
SHERYL:	As I was leaving, I saw all the pearls from the necklace rolling around on the floor. So, I had to get the dustpan and brush. I couldn't risk any of them slipping over on them.
LEANNE:	So, what about the sleeping arrangements?

SHERYL:	Luckily, Maude suddenly woke up and shouted from the bathroom, [*Old lady's voice*] "I would rather sleep in the bath, than see Edna again. So, the other two can have the beds". The other three ladies were in the room next door. Do you think they offered to help?
LEANNE:	Did they?
SHERYL:	No!!
LEANNE:	Well, what a story!
SHERYL:	I'm not even going to tell you about Mr and Mrs Grockle!!
	[EUGENE GROCKLE *appears, singing "We're caught in a trap".*]
SHERYL:	Looks like he can tell you himself. I'll go and check the bar area.
	[SHERYL *exits.*]
EUGENE:	Well, howdy little mama!
LEANNE:	Oh, hello, Mr Grockle, is it?
EUGENE:	Eugene is fine! Only Aaron Graceland, when I'm on stage!
LEANNE:	Will Mrs Grockle be joining us?
EUGENE:	I think that will not be possible. You see, she unknowingly drank some bubble bath and is burping up a huge amount of bubbles!
LEANNE:	Oh dear, how awful.
EUGENE:	She's now resting waiting for Al.
LEANNE:	Al?
EUGENE:	Yes, Sheryl said she would send Al, to make her feel better, is he a doctor?
LEANNE:	I don't know any Al, are you sure she said Al?
EUGENE:	I remember, she said she would bring up Al Catselser.
LEANNE:	Oh no, that's a tablet to settle the stomach.

EUGENE: Oh, dear lord! I see. We saw the tablets, I thought they were bath bombs to replace the bubble bath! Oh well, I don't think she'll be having a bath any time soon. I'll just let her rest. I don't think I can rest, I ended up drinking all the coffee that Sheryl brought to the room. You could say [*He sings*] "I'm all shook up".

LEANNE: I must say, I do like your outfit.

EUGENE: Elvis wore one just the same on his Vegas tour in 73.

LEANNE: Would you mind if I took some photos of you? I'm studying photography at college.

EUGENE: Not at all. I have a variety of Elvis poses! 1.The dragon pose. 2.The sultry look. 3. The highflyer.

[EUGENE *leaps into action, twisting and turning, on the table.*]

LEANNE: Oh, my goodness. Maybe just slow down a little bit. Oh, I don't think you need to jump on the table. So, let's just start with a couple of still shots.

[*Phone rings, indoor ring.*

SHERYL *enters.*]

SHERYL: Leanne, the phone!

LEANNE: Just a second Sheryl, Mr Grockle is in the most perfect light.

SHERYL: I'll answer it then! Hello, reception... Ok, calm down Maude. Has she tried jigging the lock? No that's rock around the clock.

[EUGENE *starts singing "Rock around the clock".*]

SHERYL: No, stop singing! Don't try to force the lock... No, ok. I'll come up. No, don't try and ram the door with your stick, no. Put the walking frame down... and the lamp. Just!!... Wait there and don't touch anything I'm coming up! [*Puts the phone down*] Give me strength!

[BOVEY TRACEY *appears from the arras.*]

BOVEY: Good evening most wonderful ladies.

SHERYL:	Good evening Mr Tracey... Have you had a good afternoon?
BOVEY:	Oh indeed, I had a wonderful juice in the breakfast room with Mrs Hills, I must say I gained a lot of useful knowledge from such a precocious mature lady.
SHERYL:	Glad to hear it. Leanne will look after you! I just need to rescue an old lady in the toilet!
BOVEY:	Good evening Linda.
LEANNE:	It's Leanne.
BOVEY:	I believe a complimentary aperitif is scheduled at precisely 19:00 hours.
LEANNE:	Absolutely Mr Tracey. For all our guests... Let me introduce you. This is Mr Grockle.
EUGENE:	Why, I'm happy to meet you.
BOVEY:	Yes, I'm sure you are!
	[LEANNE *continues to take photos.*
	Awkward Pause.]
EUGENE:	Real storm out there!!! It's like we're ship wrecked! On our own little Island!
BOVEY:	It reminds me of *the Tempest*!
EUGENE:	Is that a rock band, I'm not up on English groups.
BOVEY:	Oh, my dear man! *The Tempest* one of Shakespeare's works.
	Prospero uses magic to conjure a storm and torment the survivors of a shipwreck.
EUGENE:	Torment?
BOVEY:	The King's young son Ferdinand, thought to be dead, falls in love with Prospero's daughter Miranda.
EUGENE:	Miranda?
BOVEY:	Something *here* earlier caused me great concern! It reminds me of Prospero as he confronts his brother

and reveals his identity. I feel the identity of a certain guest needs to be revealed.

EUGENE: Well, you do know, I'm just the performer Aaron Graceland. I do know I'm not the real Elvis!!

BOVEY: "Might I but through my prison once a day
Behold this maid. All corners else o' the' earth
Let liberty make use of. Space enough.
Have I in such a prison"

EUGENE: I don't understand a word you said, apart from the word prison. That reminds me of a song!

[EUGENE *starts to sing 'Jail house rock'. He continues when* PADDY *and* TONY *return.* TONY *has a large plain plastic carrier bag with him.*

PADDY *and* TONY *enter, quite merry. They are singing "It's a long way to Tipperary!"*]

PADDY: It's a long way to Tipperary.

EUGENE: [*Continues to sing.*]

Dancin' to the Jailhouse Rock
Dancin' to the Jailhouse Rock
Dancin' to the Jailhouse Rock

TONY: Jail house, Oh no I'm! ...

PADDY: I'm Paddy, pleased to meet you and this is my friend Tony.

EUGENE: How do ya do?

PADDY: Grand!!

EUGENE: I'm Eugene Grockle!!

BOVEY: Good evening again Anthony. Good evening Patrick.

PADDY: Pleased to meet ya...

[LEANNE *takes photos of* PADDY *and* TONY.]

TONY: What's with all the photos?

LEANNE: Oh, it's just a hobby. You don't mind, do you?

TONY: Suppose not.

[*Meanwhile,* LEANNE *puts the photos on the front desk.*]

LEANNE: If you would excuse me, I will leave the photos here. I'm just going to get the drinks.

[*Exits*]

BOVEY: How – pray tell – do you know each other?

TONY: We met inside….

PADDY: In cid…er. We worked in a cider factory together.

BOVEY: Oh, really where was that?

[PADDY *and* TONY *speak together.*]

TONY: Hackney.

PADDY: Drangan… Yes Hackney, in… Drangan Street.

BOVEY: I see!

TONY: To be honest we got so drunk on it; we didn't know where we was half the time!!

EUGENE: Now I have heard of cider! Now that is interesting! Because apple cider in the United States is an unsweetened, non-alcoholic beverage made from apples.

PADDY: Well, is that so? Anyway Tony, you wanted to go upstairs for something, isn't that right? Take your bag with ya.

TONY: No, I don't need to go upstairs.

PADDY: Yes, you do!! Remember you had the *"cabbage soup"*.

TONY: Cabbage soup?

PADDY: Yes, the cabbage soup!! It didn't agree with you. So, you need to go upstairs and change…

TONY: Oh yes!! The *'cabbage soup'* I shall go upstairs and tell you when the *'cabbage soup'* has been deposited. I mean when I have made the *change*, erm when I have changed.

[TONY *exits*]

EUGENE: What a head scratcher! Who would have thought English was such a puzzling language!!!

PADDY: I err... think I left my keys in the er... breakfast room this morning, when I made a coffee. I'll go and check.

[*Exits*]

EUGENE: He's a real character!

BOVEY: I very much doubt he has ever consumed a hot beverage, caffeinated or otherwise. The odour of alcohol has scented the room.

Not a John Collins Bourbon Whiskey Highball, merely a cheap imitation...

EUGENE: I have no idea what you just said. I must say I do not approve of the term cheap imitation, but that man definitely is full of liquor!! I'm getting drunk just being near him!

BOVEY: Indeed, there is a time and a place for a little tipple, it is knowing when to stop that can be an issue.

[PADDY *returns*]

EUGENE: Did you find them?

PADDY: Did I find what?

EUGENE: Your keys?

PADDY: Oh no, I did not!

[*Lights go out*]

EUGENE: Who turned off the lights?

[*A crash is heard from the other room. Glasses are heard smashing.*]

BOVEY: Nobody move. It is very dangerous to move around in the dark. Oh, my darling Linda are you alright?

LEANNE: It's Leanne, yes, I'm ok. Don't come in here, there's glass everywhere. Don't worry, I have a torch on my phone. I'll be ok.

BOVEY: Maybe a fuse has blown... If only...

PADDY: I'll take a look, hold on.

[*Exits*]

EUGENE: I wouldn't know where to look for a fuse!

BOVEY: Indeed. It's as if he already knew.

[PADDY *returns*]

PADDY: It doesn't seem to be the fuse. Oh, well I think we just need to sit here, and they will probably come on very soon.

[TONY *creeps downstairs.* PADDY *sees him and sits the three of them down on the sofa.*]

PADDY: Let's all sit close and face this way.

EUGENE: Why?

BOVEY: This is extremely close!

PADDY: Because I think it may be the presence of a ghost!

EUGENE: A ghost?

PADDY: Yes, that of Molly Malone... she wheels her wheelbarrow.

[TONY *picks up the music box and it plays a tune.*]

PADDY: And her music box.

[TONY *shuts it*]

PADDY: Yes, she wheels her wheelbarrow and music box through streets broad and narrow, singing cockles and muscles alive, alive, oh! *Continues the whole song.*

BOVEY: Preposterous! I hardly think a song based on a fictional tale of a fishwife who plied her trade on the streets of Dublin in the 17th century is haunting us in Torquay!

If we are going to believe a story of ghostly hauntings, at least make it a character from William Shakespeare's play *Hamlet*. The ghost of Hamlet's father would be more apt!

EUGENE: Or Elvis!

BOVEY: Molly Malone is typically represented as a hawker by day and part-time lady of the night. Torquay is far too civilised to have a ghost of that nature.

PADDY: My ma saw the ghost many years ago. She spoke to her!

EUGENE: What did she say?

[TONY *suddenly says the code words.* (Integrate with Tony speech?)]

TONY: It's all good. The real one is as good as my pizza.

PADDY: For the love of God!!

TONY: Sorry, I didn't mean to make you jump... I was just telling you that...

EUGENE: This must have been how Elvis felt on that fateful day. Oh, my heart!!

PADDY: I'll go and try the fuse box again.

[*The lights come on*]

EUGENE: Praise the lord, I see the light!

[LEANNE *appears with a dustpan and brush*]

TONY: That's a relief!

LEANNE: All cleared up, anyone for a drink?

[BOVEY, PADDY *and* EUGENE *raise their hands*]

ALL: Yes!!

Act 3

8 a.m. Next morning.

SHERYL: Good morning Hamlet Inn. Torbay... Oh Steve. Look I told you love. We had a power cut at the hotel. Yes, I read your note. My pork balls are cold and your egg foo yung has dried up and I've gone to bed. What could I do, I was in complete darkness in a small room full of seniors? I tried to leave in the darkness, but they seemed quite scared of the dark. So then, they gave me a rendition of their Christmas concert. In July! When the lights finally came on, they still didn't want me to leave, they were doing a medley of all the songs as a grand finale. And they were convinced that Bill Cosby sang "White Christmas" and that George Michael – not Wham – sang "Last Christmas". Oh, and then one of them kept singing "Mabel it's cold outside" instead of "Baby"!! Then they tried naming all the reindeers! And since when was it "O, little town of Birmingham"? Three times I said Bethlehem and then Violet chirped in, yes, bless them all! So, think yourself lucky! [*Pause*] I told you, I'd left my phone behind the desk! You were worried? [*Pause*] I was worried, I could still be there now!

We've run out of soy sauce. Oh, so were you worried? Or just wanting to get me to bring home soy sauce? Oh, I see. [*Pause*] No, I don't have it hidden, I only do that with the crisps, you know what you're like. [*Pause*] Oh, you went out and bought some yourself. I hope that wasn't too strenuous for you. So why didn't you eat the Chinese...? You were too worried about me to eat.

So, then I had to check all the other guests were ok and help Leanne clean up the glasses. I've never seen whiskey drunken from pint glasses! The Elvis Impersonator went off singing "All shook up". Two were trying to leapfrog over each other and Mr Tracey decided to do a talk about his latest book! It was horrendous. So, that's why I was in late. Yes, I know it was gone 11! Yes, you were dead to the world this morning! That's what six beers on an empty stomach will do to you! [*Pause*] because you left them on the table! With all the food! I'm sorry your Chinese got cold. I really wanted us to have it together! It's in the fridge now, we can heat it up tonight. Alright, listen I'd better go. I have guests coming down for breakfast.

EUGENE: Well, good morning little mamma.

SHERYL: Good morning Mr Grockle. Will your wife be joining you for breakfast?

EUGENE: I'm afraid we need to check out.

SHERYL: Oh really. I have you booked in for another night. Isn't your show on tonight?

EUGENE: It was, but I'm afraid the show has been cancelled.

SHERYL: Oh no, why is that?

EUGENE: Well, my agent phoned this morning and said the show had been cancelled due to not having the staff to manage the production. No ushers, no stewards, no lighting crew.

SHERYL: Oh dear. The whole crew are unavailable. How is that possible?

EUGENE: That's what I said. Apparently, they are a travelling crew, providing backstage and front of house staff. Anyway, last night they all boarded the minibus, they always stay in Pagton.

SHERYL: Paignton.

EUGENE: The crew didn't realise that their driver Ted is visually impaired and shouldn't be driving. Apparently, they have since found out that his vision has always been blurred but he knew where the Torquay theatre car

	park was on account of "The Hamlet Inn's" bright lights. As we know there was a power cut here last night and the driver kept going past the hotel. Instead, he turned at the "Crab and Tickle" bait shop. He hit the big, illuminated crab sign and knocked himself unconscious. The crew were, in the words of Elvis "All shook up" and didn't feel they could work tonight. That and the fact, 10 tonnes of fish bait exploded on top of the van. It would have been ok if the stage manager hadn't insisted on opening two of the windows for ventilation... and word has it that the whole crew now smell like the bottom of the ocean.
SHERYL:	Oh dear. I'm so sorry for you and the crew!
EUGENE:	Oh well, to be honest. Darlene will be happy to go home and have some decent food. I was always under the impression that coming to England would be like a quiet getaway, a chance to reflect on life with only the sound of birds and the rustle of leaves. A trip to Covent Garden one evening, where you may see a duke or duchess making their wat to an embassy ball, even see a young woman, who tries to sell them some flowers. [*With a strong Cockney accent*] "The difference between a lady and a flower girl is not how she behaves, but how she is treated."
SHERYL:	Yes, I think London is a bit different from how it was in *My Fair Lady*. *The Guernsey Literary and Potato Peel Pie Society* was filmed near here.
EUGENE:	Oh God, not more awful English food! You people eat potato peel?
SHERYL:	And *Antiques Roadshow*... [DARLENE *comes down the stairs. With large dark glasses.*]
DARLENE:	Antiques who? Are we talking about the ladies in the other rooms? I swear I thought I heard them singing Christmas songs! In July!! And... Mabel it's cold

outside!! Everyone knows it's, "Maybe it's cold outside".

EUGENE: How ya feeling my little angel?

DARLENE: I'm ok! Sheryl thank you for everything you did for me last night. I went out like a light!

SHERYL: Oh, that's ok, happy I could help. Would you like breakfast before you go?

DARLENE: No. Thank you kindly. Oh Eugene. When we get home, you know what I want?

EUGENE: What darling?

DARLENE: A big bowl of "Hoppin' John" and some cornbread.

EUGENE: We'll make enough to have leftovers the day after.

DARLENE: "Hoppin' John" and then "Skippin' Jenny". Sounds like heaven.

SHERYL: Ok. Safe Journey.

DARLENE: You know there was something I really liked here.

SHERYL: Really?

DARLENE: Yes, that painting. I love sunflowers. My Auntie had a whole garden of them. I used to stay with her when I was little. I loved those sunflowers and when I saw them. I thought of my Auntie. Gave me nice feelings.

SHERYL: Oh, my little treasure.

DARLENE: Yes, like a little treasure.

SHERYL: Sorry, I've just noticed below the painting. The music box, I called it my little treasure. But that isn't *my* music box.

EUGENE: You mean, it's a different music box?

DARLENE: Oh, was it worth a lot of money? Is that why you called it your little treasure?

SHERYL: No, it wasn't worth anything. Well, only sentimental value. My cat used to play with it. She passed away.

DARLENE: Oh, was she in the music box? Her ashes?

SHERYL:	No, she just used to play with it. Silly really.
DARLENE:	No, it's not silly. We buried two dogs in our back yard and a cat. It was like our own pet cemetery. Well, I do hope you find your box.
EUGENE:	Thanks for everything. You have been wonderful. I couldn't help but notice that it looks like the Irish Guy and the Guy Ritchie wanna be, have already left. Both their doors were wide open. I hope they didn't leave without paying.
SHERYL:	Oh, they must have left really early. I was here at six. No, they paid up front.
EUGENE:	Strange characters. One had a silver lunch box he carried around with him. He must have loved that lunch box.
DARLENE:	Why do you think that darlin'?
EUGENE:	I noticed it had his name on it. It said property of "Pentonville" I guess that was his surname.
SHERYL:	Erm... Well, have a safe journey home.
EUGENE:	Thank you kindly.
DARLENE:	Bye, Bye.
EUGENE:	Oh, say goodbye to Mr Tracey for me, will you? He's another strange guy. Now he did remind me of how I saw England. Like a Henry Higgins. Yes, that's it, a proper English gentleman. Elvis has left the building. [EUGENE *and* DARLENE *leave*. BOVEY *appears*.]
BOVEY:	Good morning! My delightful Sheryl.
SHERYL:	Were your ears burning, Mr Tracey?
BOVEY:	No, I always wear a hat when walking along the sea front.
SHERYL:	Mr and Mrs Grockle said to say goodbye. I trust you slept well.

BOVEY:	Oh, indeed like a babe in arms... Are you alright? You do not look your sparkling self.
SHERYL:	Oh, it's silly really. Nothing to worry about.
BOVEY:	Oh dear, I'm afraid I am also laden with some rather distasteful news.
SHERYL:	Oh dear. I am sorry to hear that!
BOVEY:	Yes, I must tell you about the events of last night.
SHERYL:	What you mean, the power cut?
BOVEY:	I'm afraid it was not just a power cut, but an act of sabotage!! I must bring to your attention, the unjust acts of two reprobates who were staying here at the hotel. They hatched a plan to create mayhem and robbery!
SHERYL:	Oh dear.
BOVEY:	Yes, let me explain myself. Yesterday afternoon. I was rather intrigued by something I heard from Mrs Hills...
	[VIOLET *appears*]
VIOLET:	Did someone mention my name?
BOVEY:	Oh Mrs Hills, impeccable timing. Do you remember what happened yesterday?
VIOLET:	I most certainly do. Maude was stuck in the facilities and Sheryl had to come and...
BOVEY:	Oh, dear not your toilet expeditions. I meant your knowledgeable speech regarding "Grinling Gibbons".
SHERYL:	Grinling who?
VIOLET:	Grinling Gibbons was an English sculptor and wood carver known for his work in England.
SHERYL:	Oh, Yes.
BOVEY:	Mrs Hills referred to his work here at the hotel. She pointed in this direction. Mrs Hills when you spoke of his work and of its value, who was sitting in the foyer? In ear shot.

VIOLET: Well, erm... That red-faced Irish man, you know the one who smelt of whiskey and his friend the menacing looking one.

BOVEY: So, to clarify. Patrick O'Doors and Anthony Pseudonym. I will let you into a secret, that isn't his real name!! And tell us again how much a Grinling Gibbons piece like this is worth?

VIOLET: £30,000.

BOVEY: During this conversation led by Mrs Hills, and unknown to anyone, I was behind the arras in the breakfast room. I overheard the entire conversation. When Mrs Hills left, they spoke of how they were going to steal the item.

SHERYL: What, the *original* music box?

BOVEY: That's what I thought at first and so did our two convicts.

VIOLET: Oh dear!! I had no idea!!

BOVEY: At about 5 p.m. I spoke to Mrs Hills. She said she needed to get out of her room, because next door sounded like an argument was happening between Edna and Maude.

VIOLET: The walls are paper thin!

SHERYL: Oh, so you did hear it!

VIOLET: Well, I... go on Mr Tracey.

BOVEY: Mrs Hills told me; it wasn't the music box that was of immense value, but in fact the frame around the painting!!

VIOLET: Indeed.

BOVEY: I had to let them carry out their plan. I couldn't accuse them, until they were off the property. So, I had to sit through their absurd code words. The ridiculous ghost story and the almost pantomime act of losing keys and tripping fuses.

	I did – however – intervene slightly. They spoke of replacing the music box with a fake one. I removed your "Treasure box" and put in its place a shabby old music box of my own which was completely worthless. I had used it occasionally to put my fountain pens in, so I was happy to cast it aside.
SHERYL:	Oh, so you still have my treasure!
BOVEY:	Yes, I have it in a safe place. I remember the story of it being your cat's favourite toy. I do listen you know, Shelia.
SHERYL:	It's... Oh never mind. I hope you didn't leave anything of value in your music box.
BOVEY:	On the contrary I left something of great value in it. One of my cards with "duped" written on it. They won't know what that means. Perhaps they may find someone to translate for them and also a photo that Leanne took of the two of them, with the words inscribed, "Do not return! We have copies of these!!"
SHERYL:	Oh, well done Mr Bovey, so, the frame is intact, my treasure box is intact, and you have solved another crime, Mr Bovey.
BOVEY:	Well, I didn't solve it! I was privy to the whole conversation. Unlike Leanne's camera I had to merely watch it develop!
VIOLET:	Oh, you are clever, Mr Tracey.
BOVEY:	Well, thank you.
VIOLET:	Let's celebrate.
BOVEY:	How about I take you two lovely ladies out for a morning milkshake? On the way I can tell you how I solved the case of the mystery milkshake parlour sabotage!
VIOLET:	Oh, perfect.
SHERYL:	Yes, I'm due a break. Let me just pick up the post. [*Rifles through*] Oh, good – a copy of the *Torbay Echo*.

VIOLET: Oh, may I have a look? I love doing the crossword!

SHERYL: Oh, and a letter for you Mr Tracey.

BOVEY: Oh, how interesting. I recognise that handwriting. It's my old chum, Brunel Woods. A fellow writer. [*He opens the letter*] Oh dear, he seems a little out of sorts!!

VIOLET: Would that be Brunel Woods, writer of *Where did I leave my pasty?*

BOVEY: Why, yes!

VIOLET: He's on the front page of the *Torquay Echo*...

[*Holds up the paper for all to see*] He's gone missing in Teignmouth!!!

Ends.

www.ingramcontent.com/pod-product-compliance
Lightning Source LLC
Chambersburg PA
CBHW030515220526
45464CB00006B/2799